Bitcoins next chapter.

Innovations and challenges ahead

Disclaimer

The information contained in this book is for informational purposes only and should not be construed as financial, investment, legal, or other professional advice. The opinions expressed in this book are those of the author and do not necessarily reflect the views of any organizations or entities mentioned herein. The author is not responsible for any actions taken based on the information presented in this book. Readers should conduct their own research and consult with a qualified professional before making any financial decisions related to Bitcoin or other cryptocurrencies. The author and publisher disclaim any liability for losses or damages incurred as a result of the information contained in this book.

Copyright Protection

Copyright © PP Publishing, 2024. All rights reserved.

No part of this book may be reproduced, distributed, or transmitted in any form or by any means, including photocopying, recording, or other electronic or mechanical methods, without the prior written permission of the publisher, except in the case of brief quotations embodied in critical reviews and certain other noncommercial uses permitted by copyright law. For permission requests, please contact the publisher at the address below.

Publisher: PP Publishing

Contents:

Chapter 1: Introduction to Bitcoin's Evolution

- The Birth of Bitcoin
- Key Milestones in Bitcoin's History
- The Rise of Cryptocurrency

Chapter 2: Technological Innovations Driving Bitcoin Forward

- The Lightning Network and Scalability Solutions
- Layer 2 Solutions and Their Impact
- Smart Contracts and Bitcoin: A New Frontier

Chapter 3: Regulatory Landscape and Its Implications

- Global Regulatory Approaches
- Impact of Regulations on Adoption
- The Future of Compliance in Bitcoin

Chapter 4: Bitcoin in the Financial Ecosystem

- Bitcoin as Digital Gold
- Institutional Adoption and Investment Trends
- Bitcoin and the Future of Banking

Chapter 5: Security Challenges and Solutions

- Cybersecurity Threats to Bitcoin
- Advances in Wallet Security
- The Role of Decentralization in Security

Chapter 6: Environmental Concerns and Sustainability

- The Energy Debate: Proof of Work vs. Proof of Stake
- Innovations in Sustainable Mining
- The Future of Eco-Friendly Cryptocurrencies

Chapter 7: Social Impact and Inclusion

- Bitcoin and Financial Inclusion
- The Role of Bitcoin in Developing Economies
- Community Initiatives and Grassroots Movements

Chapter 8: The Future of Bitcoin: Predictions and Possibilities

- Market Trends and Price Predictions
- Bitcoin's Role in a Digital Economy
- Potential Disruptions and Innovations Ahead

Chapter 9: Conclusion and Final Thoughts

- Summarizing Key Insights
- The Road Ahead for Bitcoin
- Encouraging Responsible Engagement with Bitcoin

Chapter 10: Resources for Further Exploration

- Recommended Reading
- Online Communities and Forums
- Educational Platforms and Courses

Chapter 1: Introduction to Bitcoin's Evolution

The Birth of Bitcoin

The birth of Bitcoin marks a pivotal moment in the evolution of digital currency and financial technology. Conceived in the aftermath of the 2008 financial crisis, Bitcoin emerged as a response to the growing disillusionment with traditional banking systems. The economic turmoil exposed vulnerabilities in centralized institutions, prompting a search for alternatives that could empower individuals and restore trust in financial transactions. By introducing a decentralized currency, Bitcoin sought to eliminate the need for intermediaries, enabling peer-to-peer transactions that could operate outside the control of governments and banks.

The identity of Bitcoin's creator, Satoshi Nakamoto, remains shrouded in mystery, adding an enigmatic layer to its origin story. In 2008, Nakamoto published a white paper titled "Bitcoin: A Peer-to-Peer Electronic Cash System," outlining the principles and technical framework of Bitcoin. This document not only introduced the concept of blockchain technology — a distributed ledger that ensures transparency and security — but also emphasized the importance of cryptographic proof as a means to secure transactions. The following year, Nakamoto mined the first block of Bitcoin, known as the "genesis block," which marked the official launch of the Bitcoin network and set the stage for its subsequent growth.

Bitcoin's early adoption was fueled by a small, dedicated community of cryptography enthusiasts and libertarians who shared a vision of a decentralized financial system. The first recorded transaction using Bitcoin occurred in May 2010, when a programmer paid 10,000 Bitcoins for two pizzas, a purchase that would later be immortalized as a testament to Bitcoin's humble beginnings. As interest began to grow, more individuals started mining Bitcoin and participating in the network, leading to an increase in its value and visibility. By establishing the first cryptocurrency exchange in 2010, the market began to take shape, allowing users to trade Bitcoin for fiat currencies.

Over the years, Bitcoin has evolved from a niche digital asset to a globally recognized financial instrument. Its decentralized nature has attracted attention from investors, technologists, and regulators alike, sparking debates about its potential to disrupt traditional financial systems. As Bitcoin gained traction, it also faced significant challenges, including scalability issues, regulatory scrutiny, and security concerns. These challenges have prompted ongoing innovations within the cryptocurrency space, including developments in blockchain technology, solutions for transaction speed, and frameworks for regulatory compliance.

Today, Bitcoin stands at a crossroads, as it continues to evolve amidst a rapidly changing technological landscape. With an increasing number of businesses accepting Bitcoin as a form of payment and institutional interest on the rise, its potential as a mainstream currency is being tested. However, the future of Bitcoin is not without obstacles. The cryptocurrency market remains volatile, and debates over environmental concerns related to energy-intensive mining processes persist. As Bitcoin navigates these challenges, its journey will undoubtedly influence the broader narrative of digital currencies and shape the financial landscape for generations to come.

Key Milestones in Bitcoin's History

Bitcoin's journey began in 2008 with the publication of a white paper titled "Bitcoin: A Peer-to-Peer Electronic Cash System" by an anonymous individual or group using the pseudonym Satoshi Nakamoto. This document outlined a revolutionary concept: a decentralized digital currency that would allow for direct transactions between users without the need for intermediaries like banks. The white paper addressed issues such as double-spending and transaction verification through a mechanism known as blockchain technology. This foundational moment set the stage for what would become a financial revolution, challenging traditional notions of currency and trust in financial systems.

The first practical implementation of Bitcoin occurred in January 2009 when Nakamoto mined the genesis block, also known as Block 0. This block contained a reward of 50 bitcoins and embedded in its code was a message referencing a headline from The Times: "Chancellor on brink of second bailout for banks." This message highlighted the motivation behind Bitcoin's creation—a response to the 2008 financial crisis and a desire for a monetary system free from central bank control. In the following months, Bitcoin began to attract attention from tech enthusiasts and early adopters who recognized the potential of this new digital currency.

A significant milestone in Bitcoin's history occurred in 2010 when the first real-world transaction using Bitcoin took place. A programmer named Laszlo Hanyecz famously paid 10,000 bitcoins for two pizzas, marking the first time Bitcoin was used to purchase a tangible good. This event not only showcased Bitcoin's utility as a medium of exchange but also demonstrated its growing acceptance among the public. As more individuals began to use Bitcoin, its value began to fluctuate, paving the way for the establishment of cryptocurrency exchanges that would allow users to buy and sell Bitcoin for fiat currencies.

In 2013, Bitcoin reached a new level of visibility and legitimacy when it was featured in a segment on the popular news program "60 Minutes." This media exposure coincided with a surge in Bitcoin's price, which crossed the $1,000 mark for the first time. The increasing interest from both investors and mainstream media led to a wave of innovation within the cryptocurrency ecosystem, including the rise of alternative cryptocurrencies (altcoins) and the development of blockchain technology for various applications beyond currency. However, with increased attention came scrutiny, and regulatory discussions around Bitcoin and other cryptocurrencies began to heat up, highlighting both the potential and the challenges of this nascent technology.

By 2017, Bitcoin had solidified its position as the leading cryptocurrency, reaching an all-time high of nearly $20,000 in December of that year. This surge in price attracted a new wave of investors, including institutional players, further legitimizing Bitcoin as a viable asset class. However, the rapid rise was accompanied by significant volatility and growing concerns over security and regulatory issues. The introduction of Bitcoin futures contracts by major exchanges signaled a maturation of the market, but also foreshadowed the challenges that lay ahead, including increased regulatory scrutiny and debates over the environmental impact of Bitcoin mining. As Bitcoin moves into its next chapter, understanding these key milestones is essential for grasping the complexities and innovations that will shape its future.

The Rise of Cryptocurrency

The rise of cryptocurrency represents a significant shift in the financial landscape, initiated by the introduction of Bitcoin in 2009. This digital currency emerged as a response to the global financial crisis of 2008, when trust in traditional banks and financial institutions was severely shaken. Bitcoin's decentralized nature, operating on a technology called blockchain, offered a transparent and secure alternative to conventional currencies. This foundational innovation laid the groundwork for an entire ecosystem of cryptocurrencies, each attempting to solve unique problems or improve upon Bitcoin's framework.

Following Bitcoin's success, thousands of alternative cryptocurrencies, or altcoins, were created, each with distinct features and use cases. Ethereum, for instance, introduced the concept of smart contracts, allowing developers to create decentralized applications (daps) that operate on its blockchain. This innovation expanded the potential of cryptocurrencies beyond mere transactions, fostering a new wave of technological advancements. As these altcoins gained traction, they fueled a growing interest in the broader cryptocurrency market, attracting both retail and institutional investors who began to explore the potential for profit and diversification.

The rise of cryptocurrency has also been marked by the emergence of initial coin offerings (ICOs) and decentralized finance (DeFi). ICOs provided a novel fundraising mechanism for startups, enabling them to raise capital by issuing tokens directly to investors. DeFi platforms, on the other hand, sought to recreate traditional financial services—such as lending, borrowing, and trading—without the need for intermediaries. These developments not only demonstrated the versatility of blockchain technology but also highlighted the potential for a more inclusive financial system, particularly for those who have been underserved by traditional banking.

Regulatory scrutiny has accompanied the explosive growth of cryptocurrency, as governments and financial authorities grapple with how to manage this new asset class. Concerns over fraud, money laundering, and the volatility of cryptocurrencies have prompted calls for clearer regulations. Some countries have embraced cryptocurrencies, developing frameworks that promote innovation while ensuring consumer protection. Others have taken a more cautious approach, imposing strict regulations or outright bans. The evolving regulatory environment will play a crucial role in shaping the future of cryptocurrency, influencing its adoption and integration into mainstream finance.

In conclusion, the rise of cryptocurrency signifies not only a technological revolution but also a cultural shift towards decentralization and empowerment in finance. As the market matures, the focus will likely shift from speculation to the practical applications of blockchain technology, particularly in areas such as supply chain management, digital identity verification, and cross-border transactions. The challenges of regulation, security, and scalability remain, but the innovations driven by the cryptocurrency movement continue to push the boundaries of what is possible, setting the stage for Bitcoin's next chapter and the broader evolution of digital assets.

Chapter 2: Technological Innovations Driving Bitcoin Forward

The Lightning Network and Scalability Solutions

The Lightning Network has emerged as a groundbreaking solution designed to address one of the most pressing challenges facing Bitcoin: scalability. As Bitcoin's popularity has surged, so too have the demands placed on its underlying blockchain infrastructure. Transaction fees have risen, and confirmation times have lengthened, which can deter users and hinder the cryptocurrency's potential as a medium of exchange. The Lightning Network aims to alleviate these issues by enabling off-chain transactions that can be settled later on the main blockchain, thereby allowing for faster, cheaper, and more efficient transactions.

At its core, the Lightning Network operates by creating a network of payment channels between users. These channels enable participants to transact without the need for every transaction to be recorded on the Bitcoin blockchain. Instead, users can make multiple transactions instantly and privately, with only the opening and closing of the payment channel being recorded on-chain. This approach significantly reduces the load on the Bitcoin network and allows for millions of transactions to occur per second, a feat that the traditional blockchain could never achieve alone.

One of the key advantages of the Lightning Network is its ability to enhance user experience. As transaction times and costs decrease, individuals and businesses are more likely to adopt Bitcoin for everyday transactions. This is particularly important for small purchases, where high fees can make using Bitcoin impractical. By facilitating microtransactions, the Lightning Network not only broadens Bitcoin's usability but also reinforces its role as a viable alternative to traditional payment systems, which often involve lengthy processing times and significant fees.

However, the Lightning Network is not without its challenges. One of the primary concerns is the complexity of setting up and managing payment channels, which can be daunting for average users. Additionally, the network's reliance on a robust infrastructure of participants means that its effectiveness is contingent on widespread adoption. If only a small number of users engage with the Lightning Network, its potential benefits may not be fully realized. Furthermore, security issues, such as the risk of channel closure or the potential for funds to be locked in channels, necessitate ongoing development and user education to mitigate risks.

As Bitcoin continues to evolve, the Lightning Network represents just one of many scalability solutions being explored by the community. Other proposals, such as Segregated Witness (SegWit) and sharding, aim to improve transaction throughput and efficiency in different ways. The collective efforts to enhance Bitcoin's capabilities are critical to its long-term viability as a decentralized currency. By addressing scalability challenges head-on, innovations like the Lightning Network not only pave the way for a more efficient Bitcoin ecosystem but also ensure that Bitcoin remains relevant in an increasingly digital and fast-paced world.

Layer 2 Solutions and Their Impact

Layer 2 solutions represent a significant advancement in the scalability and efficiency of Bitcoin, addressing one of the major challenges that the network faces: transaction speed and cost. As Bitcoin's popularity has surged, so too has the volume of transactions being processed. This increase has led to congestion on the Bitcoin blockchain, resulting in slower processing times and higher transaction fees. Layer 2 solutions aim to alleviate these issues by enabling transactions to occur off the main blockchain, while still maintaining the security and decentralization that Bitcoin users value.

One of the most well-known Layer 2 solutions is the Lightning Network. This protocol allows users to create payment channels between themselves, enabling instantaneous transactions without the need for each transaction to be recorded on the Bitcoin blockchain. By aggregating multiple transactions into a single on-chain transaction, the Lightning Network significantly reduces the load on the primary blockchain. This not only speeds up transaction times but also lowers fees, making microtransactions feasible and opening new avenues for commerce and everyday use of Bitcoin.

The impact of Layer 2 solutions extends beyond mere transaction efficiency. They foster a more user-friendly experience, making Bitcoin more accessible to a broader audience. As transaction fees decrease and speed increases, the utility of Bitcoin as a medium of exchange is enhanced. This could encourage businesses to adopt Bitcoin for everyday transactions, ultimately driving greater acceptance and integration into the global economy. As more people engage with Bitcoin in practical terms, it strengthens the network's legitimacy and positions it as a viable alternative to traditional fiat currencies.

Moreover, Layer 2 solutions contribute to the overall security of the Bitcoin network. By reducing congestion on the main blockchain, they allow for better transaction verification and help maintain network integrity. Additionally, these solutions introduce innovative mechanisms for managing smart contracts and complex transaction types, broadening the range of applications for Bitcoin. As developers continue to explore the potential of Layer 2 technologies, they may unlock new capabilities that further enhance Bitcoin's functionality and appeal.

In summary, Layer 2 solutions are reshaping the landscape of Bitcoin, addressing critical challenges while simultaneously enhancing its usability and security. Their introduction marks a pivotal moment in the evolution of Bitcoin, potentially leading to increased adoption and a more robust ecosystem. As the technology matures, it will be essential for stakeholders to stay informed and engaged with these developments, as they hold the promise of transforming Bitcoin from a store of value into a dynamic medium of exchange. The future of Bitcoin may hinge on the successful implementation and widespread acceptance of Layer 2 solutions, making them a crucial area of focus for anyone invested in the cryptocurrency's potential.

Smart Contracts and Bitcoin: A New Frontier

The emergence of smart contracts represents a significant evolution in the landscape of blockchain technology, particularly in relation to Bitcoin. Traditionally, Bitcoin has been recognized primarily as a decentralized digital currency, facilitating peer-to-peer transactions without the need for intermediaries. However, the integration of smart contracts introduces a layer of programmability that can enhance the functionality of Bitcoin beyond mere currency exchange. This new frontier invites both opportunities and challenges, redefining how users interact with the Bitcoin network and how developers can harness its potential for complex transactions.

At its core, a smart contract is a self-executing contract with the terms of the agreement directly written into code. This automation allows for conditions to be met and actions to be executed without human intervention. In the context of Bitcoin, while the original protocol was not designed with smart contracts in mind, advancements in related technologies and layer-2 solutions, such as the Lightning Network, are paving the way for more sophisticated applications. These developments could enable Bitcoin to support a variety of use cases, from decentralized finance (DeFi) applications to automated escrow services, all while maintaining the security and immutability that Bitcoin is known for.

One of the most intriguing aspects of integrating smart contracts with Bitcoin is the potential for enhanced security and trust. Smart contracts eliminate the need for intermediaries, significantly reducing the risk of fraud or manipulation. By leveraging Bitcoin's robust security features, these contracts can ensure that transactions are executed exactly as programmed, instilling confidence among users. This could potentially attract a broader audience to Bitcoin, especially among those who appreciate the transparency and reliability that smart contracts can offer in various sectors, including real estate, supply chain management, and financial services.

However, the integration of smart contracts with Bitcoin is not without its challenges. One major hurdle is the limited scripting language of Bitcoin compared to other platforms like Ethereum, which was designed specifically for smart contracts. This limitation can restrict the complexity of smart contracts that can be executed on the Bitcoin network. Additionally, there are concerns regarding scalability and transaction fees, which could hinder the practical implementation of these contracts in real-world scenarios. As developers work to overcome these obstacles, the future of Bitcoin as a platform for smart contracts will depend on innovative solutions that enhance its capabilities while maintaining its core principles.

In conclusion, the intersection of smart contracts and Bitcoin represents an exciting opportunity for innovation within the blockchain ecosystem. As the technology matures, it holds the potential to revolutionize how we think about contracts, transactions, and trust. This evolution could not only broaden Bitcoin's utility but also solidify its position as a leader in the digital currency space. By embracing the potential of smart contracts, Bitcoin can navigate the challenges ahead, enabling a new era of decentralized applications and financial services that align with the ethos of its founding principles.

Chapter 3: Regulatory Landscape and Its Implications

Global Regulatory Approaches

Global regulatory approaches to Bitcoin and other cryptocurrencies vary significantly across jurisdictions, reflecting differing perspectives on innovation, consumer protection, and financial stability. As Bitcoin continues to gain traction, governments and regulatory bodies are grappling with how to effectively integrate this digital asset into their existing frameworks. The complexities of establishing a cohesive set of regulations are compounded by the decentralized nature of Bitcoin, which operates independently of any central authority. This subchapter delves into the diverse regulatory landscapes across the globe, highlighting the challenges and opportunities that arise as nations attempt to navigate the rapidly evolving cryptocurrency ecosystem.

In the United States, regulatory oversight is primarily provided by a patchwork of federal and state agencies. The Securities and Exchange Commission (SEC) and the Commodity Futures Trading Commission (CFTC) play pivotal roles in determining how Bitcoin is classified and treated under existing laws. While some states have embraced Bitcoin, offering a more favorable regulatory environment, others have imposed stringent measures aimed at preventing fraud and protecting consumers. This inconsistency can create confusion for businesses and investors alike, underscoring the need for a more unified approach to regulation that balances innovation with safety.

In contrast, countries like El Salvador have taken a bold stance by adopting Bitcoin as legal tender, a move that challenges traditional economic models and regulatory frameworks. This pioneering approach has sparked significant interest and debate, as other nations observe the outcomes of such a radical policy shift. While proponents argue that embracing Bitcoin can drive financial inclusion and economic growth, critics raise concerns about volatility and potential risks to national economies. This divergence in regulatory philosophy illustrates the varied interpretations of Bitcoin's role in the global financial landscape.

European nations have also adopted diverse regulatory strategies, with the European Union working towards a comprehensive framework that addresses the complexities of cryptocurrencies. The Markets in Crypto-Assets (MiCA) regulation aims to provide a standardized approach, promoting innovation while ensuring consumer protection and market integrity. The EU's cautious yet proactive stance reflects an understanding that regulation must evolve alongside technological advancements, fostering an environment where cryptocurrencies can thrive without compromising financial stability.

As Bitcoin's adoption continues to grow, the need for international cooperation and harmonization of regulations becomes increasingly apparent. The fragmented nature of current regulatory approaches can hinder innovation, create barriers to entry for new players, and complicate cross-border transactions. Efforts by organizations such as the Financial Action Task Force (FATF) to establish global standards for anti-money laundering and counter-terrorism financing in the cryptocurrency space underscore the importance of collaboration among nations. The future of Bitcoin will likely depend on the ability of regulators to find common ground, ensuring that the benefits of this transformative technology can be realized while minimizing potential risks.

Impact of Regulations on Adoption

The adoption of Bitcoin and other cryptocurrencies has been significantly influenced by regulatory frameworks established across different jurisdictions. As governments and regulatory bodies grapple with the implications of digital currencies, their decisions can either foster an environment conducive to innovation or stifle growth through restrictive measures.
Understanding the impact of these regulations is crucial for stakeholders, including investors, developers, and users, as they navigate the evolving landscape of digital assets.

In many regions, clear regulations have provided a degree of legitimacy to Bitcoin, encouraging broader participation from institutional investors and mainstream businesses. For instance, regulatory clarity around the classification of cryptocurrencies can lead to increased adoption by financial institutions, which may feel more secure in integrating Bitcoin into their offerings. Countries that have implemented comprehensive regulations often see a surge in cryptocurrency exchanges and related services, as companies seek to comply with legal standards while catering to a growing market of digital asset users.

Conversely, overly stringent regulations can hinder adoption by creating barriers to entry for new participants. In some cases, governments have enacted laws that impose heavy compliance burdens on cryptocurrency businesses. These regulations can discourage innovation and lead to a reduction in the number of startups entering the market. A restrictive regulatory environment can also drive users underground or to unregulated markets, where risks are higher and consumer protections are minimal. The challenge lies in finding a balance that protects consumers without stifling the entrepreneurial spirit that drives the cryptocurrency sector.

Additionally, the global nature of Bitcoin presents unique regulatory challenges. Different countries have varying approaches to cryptocurrencies, leading to a fragmented regulatory landscape. This inconsistency can create confusion and uncertainty for users and businesses operating across borders. For instance, a company that complies with regulations in one jurisdiction may find itself at odds with the laws of another, complicating international transactions and trade. As Bitcoin continues to gain traction globally, the need for harmonized regulations becomes increasingly important to facilitate seamless cross-border adoption.

Looking ahead, the evolution of regulations will play a pivotal role in shaping the future of Bitcoin. Policymakers must consider the implications of their decisions, balancing the need for consumer protection with the desire to foster innovation. By engaging with stakeholders from the cryptocurrency community, regulators can develop frameworks that support the growth of digital assets while addressing legitimate concerns. As the regulatory landscape matures, its impact on Bitcoin adoption will likely be profound, influencing everything from investment strategies to technological advancements within the ecosystem.

The Future of Compliance in Bitcoin

As the world increasingly embraces digital currencies, the future of compliance in Bitcoin presents both opportunities and challenges. The rapid evolution of regulatory frameworks is essential to ensure that Bitcoin can flourish while also safeguarding against illicit activities. Governments and regulatory bodies are beginning to recognize the need for a balanced approach that fosters innovation while protecting consumers and the financial system. This subchapter explores the potential developments in compliance practices within the Bitcoin ecosystem, considering advancements in technology, regulatory adaptations, and international cooperation.

One significant trend shaping the future of compliance in Bitcoin is the integration of advanced technologies such as artificial intelligence and machine learning. These technologies can enhance the ability of compliance programs to monitor transactions in real-time, identify suspicious activities, and streamline reporting processes. By leveraging sophisticated algorithms, companies can analyze vast amounts of data to detect patterns indicative of money laundering or fraud, thereby improving the overall integrity of the Bitcoin network. As these technologies become more widely adopted, businesses operating in the Bitcoin space will likely find themselves better equipped to meet regulatory requirements and minimize risks.

Regulatory bodies are also evolving their approaches to compliance as they gain a deeper understanding of Bitcoin and its underlying blockchain technology. Future regulations may focus on establishing clear guidelines for key players within the ecosystem, including exchanges, wallet providers, and initial coin offerings (ICOs). This clarity will help businesses operate within a well-defined legal framework, reducing uncertainty and fostering confidence among investors. Moreover, regulators may adopt a more collaborative stance, engaging with industry stakeholders to co-create standards that promote innovation while ensuring consumer protection.

International cooperation will play a vital role in shaping compliance standards for Bitcoin. As cryptocurrencies transcend borders, the need for a harmonized regulatory approach becomes increasingly apparent. Global organizations, such as the Financial Action Task Force (FATF), are already working to establish guidelines that member countries can implement to combat money laundering and terrorist financing in the cryptocurrency sector. Future developments may lead to more unified regulations across jurisdictions, which would benefit businesses by reducing compliance burdens and creating a level playing field. Enhanced collaboration among countries will also facilitate information sharing, allowing for more effective tracking of illicit activities.

Finally, the evolving landscape of compliance will likely influence the way Bitcoin is perceived by the general public. As regulatory frameworks become more robust and transparent, consumers may gain increased confidence in using Bitcoin for everyday transactions. This perception shift could drive wider adoption and encourage traditional financial institutions to explore Bitcoin-related services. Ultimately, the future of compliance in Bitcoin is not just about meeting regulatory demands; it is about building a trustworthy ecosystem that fosters innovation and protects users. As the industry moves forward, maintaining a proactive stance on compliance will be crucial for the sustained growth and success of Bitcoin in the global financial landscape.

Chapter 4: Bitcoin in the Financial Ecosystem

Bitcoin as Digital Gold

Bitcoin has often been likened to gold, and this comparison has gained traction as the cryptocurrency matures and evolves. The concept of Bitcoin as "digital gold" derives from its potential to serve as a store of value, much like precious metals. While traditional gold has been revered for centuries as a hedge against inflation and a safe haven during economic uncertainty, Bitcoin offers a modern alternative that leverages technology to enhance its appeal. This analogy is particularly relevant in discussions about the future of finance, as it encapsulates the growing recognition of Bitcoin's role in a rapidly changing economic landscape.

One of the primary reasons Bitcoin is compared to gold is its scarcity. Unlike fiat currencies, which can be printed in unlimited quantities, Bitcoin has a capped supply of 21 million coins, making it deflationary by nature. This scarcity is built into the protocol, with new bitcoins being mined at a decreasing rate over time, a process known as halving. This characteristic mirrors gold's finite supply, which makes both assets appealing to investors looking to protect their wealth against inflation. As global economies grapple with rising debt levels and currency devaluation, Bitcoin's fixed supply positions it as a potential safeguard for individuals seeking to preserve their purchasing power.

In addition to its scarcity, Bitcoin's decentralized nature further strengthens its comparison to gold. Just as gold cannot be easily manipulated or controlled by any single entity, Bitcoin operates on a peer-to-peer network that is maintained by a global community of miners and nodes. This decentralization reduces the risk of government interference or centralized control, appealing to those who value financial sovereignty. As trust in traditional financial systems wanes, Bitcoin offers an alternative that empowers individuals to hold and transfer wealth without relying on intermediaries, making it an attractive option for those disillusioned with conventional banking practices.

Moreover, Bitcoin has demonstrated resilience and adaptability in the face of market volatility, mirroring the historical performance of gold during economic downturns. While both assets can experience significant price fluctuations, Bitcoin's long-term trajectory has shown a remarkable capacity for recovery and growth. As institutional adoption increases and major corporations begin to allocate portions of their treasury reserves to Bitcoin, its status as a legitimate asset class continues to solidify. This growing acceptance suggests that Bitcoin may not only serve as a hedge against economic instability but also as a viable investment vehicle for the future.

As we move further into the digital age, the comparison of Bitcoin to gold will likely evolve. Innovations such as the development of Bitcoin-backed financial products and services, alongside advancements in blockchain technology, may pave the way for new use cases and adoption scenarios. However, challenges remain, including regulatory scrutiny and concerns about environmental sustainability. Addressing these obstacles will be crucial for Bitcoin to realize its full potential as digital gold and to cement its place in the global financial ecosystem. The ongoing dialogue surrounding Bitcoin's role as a store of value will inevitably shape its future and the broader discourse on the evolution of money itself.

Institutional Adoption and Investment Trends

Institutional adoption of Bitcoin has gained significant momentum over recent years, signaling a transformative shift in how cryptocurrencies are perceived within the financial landscape. Initially regarded as a niche asset primarily for tech enthusiasts and speculative investors, Bitcoin has increasingly attracted the attention of institutional players, including hedge funds, family offices, and publicly traded companies. This change is largely driven by a growing recognition of Bitcoin as a legitimate asset class, characterized by its potential for diversification, inflation hedging, and as a store of value akin to digital gold.

One of the most notable trends in institutional investment is the allocation of Bitcoin onto the balance sheets of publicly traded companies. Pioneers such as MicroStrategy and Tesla have set a precedent by investing substantial sums into Bitcoin, thus legitimizing its status as a corporate treasury asset. This trend reflects a broader sentiment among institutional investors who are seeking to hedge against inflation and currency devaluation, particularly in a global economic climate marked by unprecedented monetary expansion. The strategic positioning of Bitcoin in corporate portfolios underscores its appeal as a long-term investment and a potential safeguard against economic uncertainties.

Furthermore, institutional investment in Bitcoin has been bolstered by the development of sophisticated financial products that cater to this demographic. The introduction of Bitcoin exchange-traded funds (ETFs) and futures contracts has made it easier for institutional investors to gain exposure to the cryptocurrency market without the complexities associated with direct ownership. These financial instruments not only enhance liquidity but also provide a regulated framework that appeals to risk-averse investors. As more products become available, the landscape for institutional investment will continue to evolve, further integrating Bitcoin into mainstream financial markets.

Another critical aspect of institutional adoption is the increasing interest from traditional financial institutions, such as banks and asset management firms. These entities are not only facilitating Bitcoin investments for their clients but are also exploring ways to incorporate blockchain technology into their existing operations. This trend signifies a growing acceptance of cryptocurrencies and a recognition of their potential to enhance efficiency and transparency in financial transactions. As these institutions invest in infrastructure and talent related to digital assets, they pave the way for broader acceptance and integration of Bitcoin within the established financial ecosystem.

Looking ahead, the future of institutional adoption and investment trends in Bitcoin appears promising, yet it is not without challenges. Regulatory scrutiny remains a significant concern, as governments worldwide grapple with how to best oversee this rapidly evolving market. Additionally, the volatility associated with Bitcoin poses risks that institutions must carefully evaluate. However, as education and understanding of Bitcoin continue to improve among institutional investors, it is likely that we will see sustained growth in adoption. The interplay between innovation, regulation, and market dynamics will shape the path forward, making it crucial for stakeholders to remain agile and informed in the face of this evolving landscape.

Bitcoin and the Future of Banking

The emergence of Bitcoin has prompted a fundamental re-evaluation of traditional banking systems and their roles in the modern economy. As a decentralized digital currency, Bitcoin operates independently of central banks and financial institutions, challenging established paradigms of money management and transaction processing. This shift raises important questions about the future of banking, as financial institutions grapple with the implications of a currency that allows for peer-to-peer transactions without intermediaries. As we explore the potential impacts of Bitcoin on banking, it becomes evident that this digital asset could redefine how we perceive value, trust, and financial transactions.

One of the most significant ways Bitcoin is influencing the banking sector is through the concept of decentralization. Traditional banks rely on a centralized model, where trust is placed in institutions to manage and secure deposits. In contrast, Bitcoin's blockchain technology enables a distributed ledger system that records transactions across a network of computers. This decentralization not only enhances security and transparency but also empowers individuals by giving them greater control over their financial assets. As consumers become more aware of these advantages, banks may need to adapt their services and business models to accommodate a growing demand for decentralized financial solutions.

Moreover, Bitcoin introduces the notion of financial inclusion, which is particularly relevant in developing economies where access to banking services is limited. With Bitcoin, individuals can participate in the global economy without the need for a traditional bank account. This capability can be transformative, allowing people to send and receive money across borders with minimal fees and without the bureaucratic hurdles often associated with conventional banking. As more individuals gain access to Bitcoin and similar cryptocurrencies, banks may be compelled to rethink their strategies for reaching unbanked populations and enhancing their service offerings to remain competitive.

The integration of Bitcoin into existing banking frameworks also presents both opportunities and challenges. Financial institutions are beginning to explore how they can leverage Bitcoin's underlying technology, such as blockchain, to improve their operations. Innovations like smart contracts and automated payment systems could streamline processes and reduce costs. However, these advancements also bring challenges related to regulation, security, and the potential displacement of traditional banking roles. As banks navigate this evolving landscape, they must strike a balance between embracing innovation and ensuring compliance with existing regulations to protect consumers.

In conclusion, the relationship between Bitcoin and the future of banking is complex and multifaceted. As Bitcoin continues to gain traction, it is likely to influence banking practices, reshape consumer expectations, and challenge the status quo of financial systems. Banks that recognize the potential of Bitcoin and adapt accordingly may find new avenues for growth and engagement in an increasingly digital economy. Conversely, institutions that resist change could risk obsolescence in a world where consumers are increasingly seeking autonomy and transparency in their financial transactions. The future of banking will undoubtedly be shaped by how well these institutions respond to the innovations and challenges presented by Bitcoin.

Chapter 5: Security Challenges and Solutions

Cybersecurity Threats to Bitcoin

Cybersecurity threats to Bitcoin represent a significant challenge as the cryptocurrency continues to gain traction in various sectors. As digital assets become more mainstream, understanding the vulnerabilities that accompany their use is crucial. This subchapter will explore the primary cybersecurity threats faced by Bitcoin, including hacking incidents, wallet security, phishing attacks, and the implications of quantum computing.

One of the most notable threats to Bitcoin security is hacking, particularly targeting cryptocurrency exchanges and wallets. High-profile breaches have resulted in the loss of millions of dollars' worth of Bitcoin, undermining user confidence in the security of these platforms. Attackers employ techniques such as Distributed Denial of Service (DDoS) attacks to disrupt services or exploit vulnerabilities in software to gain unauthorized access. As exchanges and wallets serve as the primary interfaces for buying, selling, and storing Bitcoin, their security measures are critical to the overall integrity of the cryptocurrency ecosystem.

Wallet security is another area of concern for Bitcoin users. Many individuals store their Bitcoin in software wallets, which are susceptible to malware and phishing attacks. Cybercriminals often deploy sophisticated tactics to trick users into revealing their private keys or login credentials, leading to the theft of funds. Hardware wallets, which provide a more secure method of storage by keeping private keys offline, are recommended for users looking to safeguard their assets. However, even hardware wallets are not immune to threats, as vulnerabilities in the devices themselves can be exploited if users do not follow best security practices.

Phishing attacks have become increasingly prevalent in the Bitcoin landscape. Cybercriminals employ deceptive emails, websites, and social media posts to lure users into providing sensitive information. These attacks can be particularly damaging because they prey on individuals' lack of familiarity with the technology. Users may mistakenly believe they are interacting with legitimate services, only to find that their information has been compromised. Education and awareness are vital in combating these threats, as users must remain vigilant and skeptical of unsolicited communications.

Looking toward the future, the rise of quantum computing poses an existential threat to Bitcoin and other cryptocurrencies. Quantum computers have the potential to break the cryptographic algorithms that underpin Bitcoin's security, potentially allowing attackers to forge transactions or compromise wallets. While practical quantum computing is still a developing field, the implications are profound. Researchers are already exploring quantum-resistant cryptographic methods, but the timeline for widespread adoption remains uncertain. As the technology evolves, it is imperative for the Bitcoin community to stay ahead of these threats to ensure the longevity and security of the network.

In summary, cybersecurity threats to Bitcoin encompass a broad range of challenges that users and developers must navigate as the cryptocurrency evolves. From hacking incidents and wallet vulnerabilities to phishing schemes and the impending threat of quantum computing, the landscape is fraught with danger. As Bitcoin continues to grow in popularity, fostering a culture of security awareness and proactive measures will be essential in mitigating these risks. By addressing these challenges head-on, the Bitcoin community can work toward a more secure future, ensuring that the innovations surrounding this digital asset can flourish without the shadow of cyber threats.

Advances in Wallet Security

The landscape of cryptocurrency has evolved significantly since Bitcoin's inception, with security becoming a paramount concern for users and developers alike. As Bitcoin gains popularity and mainstream acceptance, ensuring the safety of digital wallets is crucial for fostering trust and encouraging broader adoption. Advances in wallet security encompass a range of innovations designed to protect users from theft, hacking, and other vulnerabilities that threaten their digital assets. This subchapter will explore some of the most notable developments in wallet security and their implications for the future of Bitcoin.

One significant advancement in wallet security is the implementation of multi-signature technology. Multi-signature wallets require multiple private keys to authorize a transaction, adding an extra layer of protection against unauthorized access. This feature is particularly beneficial for businesses and organizations that manage larger amounts of Bitcoin, as it mitigates the risk of a single point of failure. By distributing control among multiple stakeholders, the likelihood of theft decreases, and accountability is enhanced. As multi-signature solutions become more user-friendly, their adoption across various sectors is expected to increase, thereby strengthening overall wallet security.

Another noteworthy innovation in wallet security is the integration of biometric authentication. With the rise of smartphones and other personal devices, biometric methods such as fingerprint scanning and facial recognition are becoming commonplace. These technologies provide a convenient and secure way for users to access their wallets while reducing the reliance on traditional passwords, which can often be weak or easily compromised. As biometric authentication continues to improve, it presents an opportunity to enhance the security of Bitcoin wallets, making them more resilient against unauthorized access and hacking attempts.

Furthermore, the development of hardware wallets has revolutionized how users store their Bitcoin. Hardware wallets are physical devices that securely store private keys offline, making them less susceptible to online threats. These wallets have gained traction among serious investors and traders who prioritize security over convenience. As technology advances, hardware wallets are becoming more sophisticated, offering features such as built-in screens, secure backup options, and compatibility with various cryptocurrencies. The continued evolution of hardware wallets is likely to play a crucial role in the future of Bitcoin security, as they provide a robust solution to the ongoing challenges of cyber threats.

Lastly, the rise of decentralized finance (DeFi) and decentralized applications (daps) has prompted advancements in wallet security protocols. As users engage with DeFi platforms, they are increasingly aware of the potential risks involved. In response, developers are creating wallets that incorporate advanced security features such as smart contract audits, transaction monitoring, and insurance options against hacks and exploits. By prioritizing security within the DeFi ecosystem, these innovations not only protect individual users but also contribute to the overall integrity and stability of the Bitcoin network.

In conclusion, the advances in wallet security reflect the ongoing commitment of the cryptocurrency community to protect users and their assets. As Bitcoin continues to evolve and integrate into the global financial system, the importance of robust security measures cannot be overstated. Innovations such as multi-signature technology, biometric authentication, hardware wallets, and enhanced DeFi protocols are paving the way for a safer and more secure future for Bitcoin. As these developments unfold, they will play a crucial role in shaping user experiences, fostering trust, and promoting the widespread adoption of Bitcoin in the years to come.

The Role of Decentralization in Security

Decentralization plays a pivotal role in enhancing security within the Bitcoin network and the broader cryptocurrency ecosystem. Unlike traditional financial systems that rely on centralized authorities, such as banks and governments, Bitcoin operates on a decentralized model that empowers individual users. This shift reduces the risk of systemic failures that can arise from a single point of control. By distributing power among numerous participants, Bitcoin minimizes the potential for fraud, manipulation, and censorship, creating a more resilient financial environment.

One of the key aspects of decentralization is its ability to enhance trust and transparency. In a decentralized network, transactions are recorded on a public ledger known as the blockchain, which is accessible to all participants. This transparency ensures that all transactions can be verified by anyone, making it exceedingly difficult for any single entity to alter transaction data without consensus from the network. As a result, users can engage in peer-to-peer transactions with a higher level of confidence, as the risks associated with trusting a centralized intermediary are significantly diminished.

Moreover, decentralization contributes to the security of users' assets. In traditional banking systems, customer funds are vulnerable to various threats, including hacking, regulatory changes, and institutional failures. In contrast, Bitcoin allows users to control their own private keys, which are essential for accessing and transferring their assets. This self-custody model empowers users to safeguard their wealth without relying on third parties. However, it also places the onus of security on the individual, highlighting the need for education and awareness about best practices in cryptocurrency management.

Decentralization also fosters innovation in security technologies. As the cryptocurrency landscape evolves, developers are continuously working on solutions to enhance the security of decentralized networks. Innovations such as multi-signature wallets, hardware wallets, and decentralized finance (DeFi) protocols are examples of how the decentralized nature of Bitcoin encourages the exploration of new security measures. These advancements not only improve the safety of individual transactions but also contribute to the overall robustness of the network, making it a more attractive option for users seeking secure financial alternatives.

Finally, the role of decentralization in security extends beyond individual transactions to encompass the network as a whole. The consensus mechanisms employed by Bitcoin, such as proof-of-work, require participants to validate transactions and maintain the integrity of the blockchain. This collective effort creates a security layer that is difficult to breach, as any attempt to manipulate the network would require an enormous amount of computational power. Consequently, decentralization not only protects individual users but also fortifies the entire Bitcoin ecosystem, ensuring its longevity and resilience against potential threats.

Chapter 6: Environmental Concerns and Sustainability

The Energy Debate: Proof of Work vs. Proof of Stake

The energy debate surrounding blockchain consensus mechanisms has become increasingly prominent as the cryptocurrency landscape evolves. Two of the most discussed methods are Proof of Work (PoW) and Proof of Stake (PoS). PoW, established by Bitcoin, requires miners to solve complex mathematical problems to validate transactions and secure the network. This process consumes substantial amounts of energy, leading to environmental concerns and discussions about sustainability. In contrast, PoS offers an alternative that relies on validators who hold and stake their cryptocurrency as collateral, significantly reducing energy consumption. Understanding the fundamental differences between these mechanisms is crucial for assessing their implications for Bitcoin's future and the broader cryptocurrency ecosystem.

At the heart of the energy debate is the environmental impact of PoW mining. Bitcoin mining operations, often powered by fossil fuels, have drawn criticism for their carbon footprint. The energy-intensive nature of PoW is exacerbated by the competitive structure of mining, where only a fraction of participants can earn rewards, pushing miners to seek out the cheapest energy sources. This has led to a paradox: Bitcoin, heralded as a decentralized and innovative financial system, is often characterized by its association with unsustainable energy practices. As awareness of climate change grows, the need for a sustainable approach to cryptocurrency is more pressing than ever.

On the other hand, PoS presents a more environmentally friendly alternative, which has gained traction among various blockchain projects. Unlike PoW, PoS does not rely on energy-intensive computations. Instead, validators are selected based on the amount of cryptocurrency they hold and are willing to "stake." This mechanism not only reduces energy consumption but also aligns the interests of validators with the network's health, as their rewards are directly tied to their investments. However, critics argue that PoS could lead to centralization, as those with greater holdings may have disproportionately more influence over the network, potentially undermining the decentralized ethos that underpins cryptocurrencies like Bitcoin.

The transition from PoW to PoS has sparked extensive debate within the cryptocurrency community. Proponents of PoW argue that its security and proven track record make it indispensable for Bitcoin, while supporters of PoS emphasize the urgent need for sustainability and scalability in the face of growing global energy concerns. This discourse often highlights the philosophical underpinnings of each system: PoW champions the meritocratic notion of effort and investment in computational resources, while PoS advocates for a more egalitarian approach that rewards those who are willing to commit their holdings to the network.

As Bitcoin navigates its next chapter, the energy debate between PoW and PoS will play a crucial role in shaping its future. Stakeholders must grapple with the implications of each mechanism, not only in terms of energy consumption but also regarding security, decentralization, and the broader impact on society. The ongoing innovations and challenges in this space will likely influence regulatory discussions, investment strategies, and the public perception of cryptocurrencies. Ultimately, finding a balance between security, sustainability, and accessibility will be essential for Bitcoin's long-term viability and relevance in an increasingly environmentally conscious world.

Innovations in Sustainable Mining

Innovations in sustainable mining have emerged as a crucial response to the growing concerns about the environmental impact of cryptocurrency mining, particularly Bitcoin. As the demand for Bitcoin continues to rise, the industry faces increasing scrutiny regarding its energy consumption and carbon footprint. Sustainable mining practices seek to address these issues by integrating advanced technologies and renewable energy sources into mining operations. This subchapter explores various innovations that have the potential to transform Bitcoin mining into an eco-friendlier endeavor while maintaining the integrity and security of the blockchain.

One of the most significant innovations in sustainable mining is the adoption of renewable energy sources. Many mining operations are now turning to solar, wind, and hydroelectric power to reduce their reliance on fossil fuels. For instance, solar farms are being developed in arid regions where sunlight is abundant, allowing miners to harness energy during peak production hours. Similarly, wind farms are being strategically placed in areas with high wind potential, enabling miners to benefit from consistent energy generation. By utilizing renewable energy, miners not only decrease their carbon emissions but also stabilize their operational costs, as renewable energy prices continue to decline.

Another noteworthy advancement is the development of more energy-efficient mining hardware. As the competition in Bitcoin mining intensifies, manufacturers are constantly innovating to create more powerful and energy-efficient mining rigs. The introduction of ASIC (Application-Specific Integrated Circuit) miners has revolutionized the industry by providing higher hash rates while consuming less power compared to traditional mining equipment. These advancements not only enhance mining efficiency but also contribute to a reduction in overall energy consumption, making sustainable mining more feasible and attractive to operators.

Additionally, innovations in cooling technologies have emerged as a vital component of sustainable mining practices. Traditional mining rigs generate significant heat, leading to increased energy consumption for cooling systems. New cooling solutions, such as immersion cooling and liquid cooling, have been developed to efficiently manage heat production while minimizing energy usage. These methods allow miners to operate their equipment at optimal temperatures without excessive energy expenditure, further contributing to the sustainability of mining operations. By adopting these advanced cooling techniques, miners can reduce their environmental impact while improving the longevity and performance of their hardware.

Finally, the integration of blockchain technology into the energy sector presents new opportunities for sustainable mining initiatives. Projects that utilize blockchain for energy trading and management enable miners to purchase excess renewable energy directly from producers, facilitating a more decentralized energy market. This innovation not only supports the growth of renewable energy sources but also encourages miners to align their operations with sustainable practices. By participating in these blockchain-based energy platforms, Bitcoin miners can contribute to a greener energy ecosystem while benefiting from cost savings and increased operational efficiency.

In conclusion, the innovations in sustainable mining represent a significant shift in the Bitcoin industry as it seeks to reconcile the growing demand for cryptocurrency with environmental responsibility. Through the adoption of renewable energy sources, energy-efficient hardware, advanced cooling technologies, and blockchain integration, mining operations can reduce their ecological footprint and contribute to a more sustainable future. As these innovations gain traction, they will play a critical role in shaping the future of Bitcoin, ensuring that it remains not only a revolutionary financial instrument but also a responsible one.

The Future of Eco-Friendly Cryptocurrencies

The landscape of cryptocurrencies is evolving rapidly, with eco-friendly alternatives gaining traction as both technology and environmental concerns converge. The future of eco-friendly cryptocurrencies is being shaped by a growing awareness of the environmental impact of traditional blockchain systems, particularly those reliant on energy-intensive proof-of-work mechanisms. As climate change becomes an increasingly pressing issue, the cryptocurrency community is recognizing the need for sustainable practices that minimize carbon footprints and promote ecological responsibility. This shift not only aims to attract environmentally conscious investors but also seeks to align the crypto industry with global sustainability goals.

Innovative consensus mechanisms are at the forefront of the development of eco-friendly cryptocurrencies. Proof of Stake (PoS) and Delegated Proof of Stake (DPoS) are two prominent alternatives to the traditional proof-of-work model. These mechanisms drastically reduce energy consumption by allowing users to validate transactions based on the number of coins they hold, rather than competing to solve complex mathematical problems. As PoS networks gain popularity, established cryptocurrencies like Ethereum are transitioning to these more sustainable models, signaling a significant shift in the industry's approach to energy consumption.

The integration of renewable energy sources in cryptocurrency mining is another avenue that has the potential to revolutionize the industry. Mining operations powered by solar, wind, or hydroelectric energy can significantly reduce the carbon footprint associated with cryptocurrency transactions. Furthermore, the emergence of specialized mining farms in regions rich in renewable energy resources is creating opportunities for sustainable growth. As the demand for green energy solutions increases, the crypto community may find itself at the forefront of promoting and implementing renewable energy technologies, ultimately benefiting both the environment and the economy.

Regulatory frameworks and public perception play crucial roles in the acceptance and growth of eco-friendly cryptocurrencies. As governments and regulatory bodies become more attuned to environmental issues, they may incentivize the adoption of sustainable practices within the crypto industry. This could take the form of tax breaks, grants, or other financial support for projects that prioritize eco-friendliness. Additionally, as consumers become more environmentally conscious, their preferences for eco-friendly options may drive demand for cryptocurrencies that prioritize sustainability, fostering an environment where green initiatives can thrive.

Looking ahead, the future of eco-friendly cryptocurrencies appears promising. As the technology matures and the demand for sustainable financial solutions rises, innovation will likely accelerate. Collaborative efforts among developers, environmental organizations, and regulatory bodies could lead to the establishment of industry standards that prioritize ecological sustainability. This collective responsibility will not only enhance the legitimacy of cryptocurrencies but also ensure that they contribute positively to the global economy and environment. In this context, eco-friendly cryptocurrencies may not only serve as viable investment options but also as catalysts for meaningful change in the financial landscape.

Chapter 7: Social Impact and Inclusion

Bitcoin and Financial Inclusion

Bitcoin, often heralded as a revolutionary financial technology, possesses the potential to significantly enhance financial inclusion across the globe. Traditional banking systems frequently overlook marginalized populations, leaving millions without access to essential financial services. Bitcoin's decentralized nature and borderless transaction capabilities create avenues for individuals who have historically been excluded from the financial system, enabling them to participate in the global economy more fully.

In many developing regions, individuals face barriers such as high fees, lack of infrastructure, and stringent identification requirements that prevent them from accessing banking services. Bitcoin offers an alternative by allowing users to create wallets and conduct transactions with minimal barriers to entry. The ability to transact without needing a traditional bank account is particularly beneficial in areas where banking infrastructure is lacking. This democratization of finance empowers individuals to store wealth, make payments, and engage in commerce without the constraints imposed by conventional financial institutions.

Moreover, Bitcoin facilitates remittances, which are vital for many families in developing countries. Traditional remittance services often charge exorbitant fees, which can consume a significant portion of the funds being sent. By using Bitcoin, senders can reduce transaction costs and avoid unfavorable exchange rates, ensuring that more money reaches the intended recipients. This efficiency not only improves the financial situation of families relying on remittances but also contributes to local economies, as recipients can invest in businesses or education.

The integration of Bitcoin into everyday transactions also fosters financial literacy among individuals who may have been previously unaware of financial management practices. As people engage with Bitcoin, they learn about concepts such as value storage, investment, and market dynamics. This newfound knowledge can encourage better financial decision-making and enhance economic resilience within communities. Furthermore, as more individuals adopt Bitcoin, there is potential for the creation of new job opportunities in sectors related to cryptocurrency, technology, and education around digital finance.

Despite the promise that Bitcoin holds for financial inclusion, challenges remain. Issues such as volatility, regulatory uncertainty, and the digital divide can hinder widespread adoption. To realize the full potential of Bitcoin as a tool for financial inclusion, stakeholders — including governments, financial institutions, and technology providers — must work collaboratively to address these hurdles. By fostering a supportive environment for Bitcoin innovation and enhancing digital literacy, society can harness the transformative power of this cryptocurrency and pave the way for a more inclusive financial future.

The Role of Bitcoin in Developing Economies

The emergence of Bitcoin has sparked considerable interest in its potential to influence developing economies. As these nations grapple with various financial challenges such as inflation, limited access to banking services, and economic instability, Bitcoin presents an alternative financial solution. By providing a decentralized and borderless form of currency, Bitcoin enables individuals in developing countries to engage in global markets, facilitating trade and investment that may otherwise be inaccessible.

One of the most significant advantages of Bitcoin in developing economies is its ability to act as a hedge against hyperinflation and currency devaluation. Many countries experience fluctuating national currencies that can lead to loss of savings and uncertainty in everyday transactions. Bitcoin, with its fixed supply cap of 21 million coins, offers a more stable store of value. Individuals can convert their local currency into Bitcoin to preserve their wealth, thereby reducing their exposure to the volatility of local financial systems. This shift not only empowers individuals but also provides a pathway for increased economic stability.

Access to banking services remains a critical issue in many developing regions, where a significant portion of the population remains unbanked or underbanked. Bitcoin's decentralized nature allows individuals to bypass traditional banking systems, enabling them to store and transfer value without the need for intermediaries. This is particularly important for those living in remote areas where banking infrastructure is scarce. By utilizing Bitcoin, individuals can transact with ease, access global markets, and participate in the digital economy, fostering entrepreneurship and innovation.

Moreover, Bitcoin can facilitate remittances, which are a vital source of income for many families in developing economies. Traditional remittance services often come with high fees and long processing times, making it challenging for families to receive funds from abroad. Bitcoin significantly reduces these costs and speeds up transaction times, allowing for quicker access to funds. This not only benefits the recipients but also encourages more individuals to send remittances, ultimately contributing to local economies and improving the quality of life.

However, the integration of Bitcoin into developing economies is not without challenges. Issues such as regulatory uncertainty, technological barriers, and fluctuating market conditions can pose significant risks. Additionally, education and awareness surrounding cryptocurrency are crucial for ensuring that individuals can use Bitcoin effectively and safely. Addressing these challenges will require collaboration between governments, tech companies, and local communities to create a supportive environment that fosters the growth of Bitcoin and its adoption in developing economies. As the world continues to evolve, the role of Bitcoin could become increasingly vital, potentially transforming the financial landscape for millions.

Community Initiatives and Grassroots Movements

Community initiatives and grassroots movements are playing an increasingly vital role in shaping the future of Bitcoin and the broader cryptocurrency landscape. As the technology matures, these local efforts are emerging as critical components in advocating for the adoption and implementation of Bitcoin. By fostering community engagement and promoting education, grassroots movements serve as a bridge between traditional financial systems and the decentralized ethos that Bitcoin embodies. This subchapter will explore various initiatives that highlight the intersection of community involvement and Bitcoin innovation, illustrating their potential to drive meaningful change.

One prominent example of community initiative is the establishment of Bitcoin education programs in underserved areas. Organizations are forming to provide free workshops, seminars, and online resources aimed at demystifying Bitcoin and equipping individuals with the knowledge to navigate the cryptocurrency space. These educational efforts are essential in breaking down barriers to entry, especially for those who may feel intimidated by complex jargon or technological concepts. By fostering a more informed populace, these initiatives help cultivate a new generation of Bitcoin advocates who can champion the benefits of decentralized finance in their communities.

Grassroots movements are also pushing for regulatory reforms that align with the principles of decentralization and user sovereignty. Activists and advocates are mobilizing to influence policymakers at local, state, and national levels to create a regulatory environment that supports innovation while protecting consumer rights. These movements often emphasize transparency, urging lawmakers to consider the unique qualities of cryptocurrencies like Bitcoin rather than applying outdated frameworks from traditional finance. By organizing campaigns, petitions, and public forums, these grassroots efforts aim to ensure that Bitcoin's future is shaped by the voices of its users rather than solely by the interests of established financial entities.

In addition to education and advocacy, community initiatives are facilitating the development of local Bitcoin economies. Various cities around the world have embraced the idea of "Bitcoin meetups," where enthusiasts gather to share knowledge, network, and promote local businesses that accept Bitcoin. These gatherings not only foster a sense of community but also encourage the practical use of Bitcoin in everyday transactions. As more businesses adopt Bitcoin as a payment method, they help to reinforce its legitimacy and utility, creating a positive feedback loop that encourages further adoption.

Lastly, the rise of community-driven projects, such as Bitcoin Circles or local mining cooperatives, exemplifies the power of collective action. These initiatives allow individuals to pool resources and share knowledge, enabling them to participate in Bitcoin mining or investment in a more manageable way. By leveraging community strength, participants can mitigate risks and enhance their understanding of the technology. This cooperative spirit not only democratizes access to Bitcoin but also strengthens community ties, illustrating the profound impact that grassroots movements can have on the cryptocurrency's evolution. As these initiatives continue to grow, they are likely to play a pivotal role in shaping Bitcoin's next chapter.

Chapter 8: The Future of Bitcoin: Predictions and Possibilities

Market Trends and Price Predictions

The landscape of Bitcoin has witnessed significant transformation since its inception, evolving from a niche digital currency to a mainstream asset class. Understanding the current market trends is crucial for investors and enthusiasts alike, as these trends serve as indicators of Bitcoin's future trajectory. Recent data reveals a growing institutional interest, with hedge funds and corporations increasingly adding Bitcoin to their portfolios. This influx of institutional capital has not only provided legitimacy to the cryptocurrency but has also stabilized its price movements, making Bitcoin a more attractive investment option amidst the volatility that has historically characterized its market.

Technological advancements within the Bitcoin ecosystem are also shaping market trends. The implementation of the Lightning Network, which aims to facilitate faster and cheaper transactions, is enhancing Bitcoin's utility as a medium of exchange. As transaction speeds improve, more merchants are likely to adopt Bitcoin, further driving its usage and demand. Additionally, improvements in security protocols and regulatory clarity are fostering a more favorable environment for Bitcoin trading and investment. These technological developments position Bitcoin not only as a store of value but also as a viable currency for everyday transactions.

Price predictions for Bitcoin remain a hot topic among analysts and market watchers. Several models have emerged, attempting to forecast Bitcoin's price based on historical data and market behavior. Notably, the Stock-to-Flow model, which correlates Bitcoin's scarcity to its value, suggests that the price may reach unprecedented heights in the coming years as halving events reduce the rate of new Bitcoin creation. While such models provide an optimistic outlook, it is essential to approach these predictions with caution, acknowledging the inherent volatility and unpredictability of cryptocurrency markets.

Furthermore, macroeconomic factors play a significant role in influencing Bitcoin's price trajectory. Global economic trends, such as inflation rates, currency devaluation, and geopolitical instability, can drive investors toward Bitcoin as a hedge against traditional financial systems. The recent uptick in inflation across various economies has led to a renewed interest in Bitcoin as a "digital gold," prompting many to view it as a safe haven asset. Consequently, changes in the global economic landscape will likely continue to affect Bitcoin's adoption and price movements.

In conclusion, while the future of Bitcoin is fraught with challenges, the prevailing market trends and price predictions paint a picture of cautious optimism. The convergence of institutional adoption, technological advancements, and macroeconomic influences suggests that Bitcoin is poised for continued growth. However, potential investors must remain vigilant, recognizing that the cryptocurrency market is still in its infancy and subject to rapid changes. As Bitcoin navigates its next chapter, understanding these dynamics will be essential for anyone looking to engage meaningfully with this revolutionary asset.

Bitcoin's Role in a Digital Economy

Bitcoin has emerged as a significant player in the landscape of digital economies, fundamentally altering how value is perceived, transferred, and stored. As a decentralized cryptocurrency, Bitcoin operates on a peer-to-peer network, allowing for direct transactions without the need for intermediaries like banks. This innovation not only reduces transaction costs but also democratizes access to financial services, particularly for individuals and businesses in regions with limited banking infrastructure. The implications of Bitcoin's rise extend far beyond mere financial transactions; it signifies a shift towards a more inclusive and efficient economic system.

One of the most compelling aspects of Bitcoin within a digital economy is its ability to serve as a store of value akin to digital gold. As traditional fiat currencies face inflationary pressures and geopolitical uncertainties, Bitcoin offers an alternative that is not subject to the same vulnerabilities. The capped supply of 21 million bitcoins creates scarcity, making it an attractive asset for investors and a potential hedge against inflation. This characteristic has garnered significant attention from institutional investors, signaling a growing acceptance of Bitcoin as a legitimate asset class that can coexist with traditional financial instruments.

Moreover, Bitcoin's underlying technology, blockchain, introduces transparency and security to transactions. Each Bitcoin transaction is recorded on a public ledger, making it nearly impossible to manipulate or counterfeit. This transparency can enhance trust in financial systems, particularly in sectors prone to fraud and corruption. As businesses and consumers become more aware of these benefits, the integration of Bitcoin into everyday transactions could lead to a broader adoption of cryptocurrencies in various industries, from e-commerce to remittances, thereby stimulating economic growth.

The role of Bitcoin in a digital economy also intersects with regulatory considerations. Governments around the world are grappling with how to approach cryptocurrencies, balancing the need for innovation with the necessity of consumer protection and financial stability. Clear regulatory frameworks can foster trust and encourage the adoption of Bitcoin, while overly restrictive measures may stifle its potential. As nations seek to harness the benefits of digital currencies, the evolution of Bitcoin's regulatory landscape will play a critical role in shaping its future and its integration into the global economy.

In conclusion, Bitcoin's role in a digital economy is multifaceted, presenting both opportunities and challenges. Its potential to revolutionize financial transactions, serve as a store of value, and enhance transparency positions it as a key player in the future of finance. However, the successful integration of Bitcoin will depend on the collaborative efforts of innovators, regulators, and the public to create a balanced framework that promotes growth while safeguarding the interests of all stakeholders. As we move forward, understanding and navigating these dynamics will be essential for realizing Bitcoin's full potential in the digital economy.

Potential Disruptions and Innovations Ahead

As Bitcoin continues to evolve within the broader financial landscape, it is essential to consider the potential disruptions and innovations that lie ahead. The cryptocurrency market is characterized by rapid changes, driven by technological advancements, regulatory developments, and shifting consumer behaviors. Understanding these dynamics is crucial for investors, policymakers, and enthusiasts alike, as they navigate the complexities of Bitcoin's future.

One of the most significant potential disruptions on the horizon is the rise of central bank digital currencies (CBDCs). As governments around the world explore the feasibility of issuing their digital currencies, the implications for Bitcoin could be profound. CBDCs may offer a state-backed alternative to decentralized cryptocurrencies, potentially leading to increased competition. However, they could also enhance the legitimacy of digital currencies overall, fostering greater public acceptance and integration into mainstream finance. The interaction between CBDCs and Bitcoin will likely shape the regulatory landscape and influence user preferences.

Another area ripe for innovation is the development of Bitcoin Layer 2 solutions, which aim to enhance scalability and transaction speed. Technologies like the Lightning Network are already making strides in facilitating faster, cheaper transactions. As these solutions mature, they could significantly reduce the barriers to Bitcoin adoption for everyday users. Enhanced usability and efficiency may attract a broader audience, including those previously hesitant to engage with cryptocurrency. This shift could lead to increased transaction volume and a more robust ecosystem around Bitcoin.

Moreover, advancements in blockchain technology itself could lead to new use cases for Bitcoin beyond mere currency. Innovations in smart contracts, interoperability between different blockchain networks, and decentralized finance (DeFi) applications are just a few examples of how Bitcoin's underlying technology could be leveraged for diverse purposes. As developers explore these possibilities, Bitcoin could transition from a digital gold narrative to a more versatile asset capable of powering various financial services. This evolution could enhance its value proposition and appeal to a wider range of investors.

Finally, the ongoing discourse surrounding environmental sustainability presents both challenges and opportunities for Bitcoin. The energy-intensive nature of Bitcoin mining has drawn criticism and sparked debates about its carbon footprint. In response, there is a growing movement within the industry to adopt more sustainable practices, including the use of renewable energy sources. Innovations aimed at reducing energy consumption and enhancing the efficiency of mining operations could mitigate these concerns, potentially positioning Bitcoin as a more environmentally friendly asset. This shift may influence public perception and regulatory approaches, ultimately impacting Bitcoin's long-term viability.

In summary, the future of Bitcoin is poised for significant disruptions and opportunities driven by technological advancements, regulatory changes, and evolving consumer preferences. Central bank digital currencies, Layer 2 solutions, innovative applications of blockchain technology, and a focus on sustainability will all play pivotal roles in shaping Bitcoin's trajectory. Understanding these factors will be essential for stakeholders aiming to navigate the complexities of Bitcoin's next chapter.

Chapter 9: Conclusion and Final Thoughts

Summarizing Key Insights

In examining the future of Bitcoin, it is essential to distil the key insights that have emerged from recent developments and ongoing discussions in the cryptocurrency space. The evolution of Bitcoin has been marked by a series of innovations and challenges that not only shape its current landscape but also influence its trajectory. Understanding these insights can provide valuable context for adults interested in navigating the complexities of Bitcoin's future.

One of the most significant insights is the growing institutional adoption of Bitcoin. Over the past few years, corporations and financial institutions have begun to recognize Bitcoin as a legitimate asset class. This shift has been driven by the increasing perception of Bitcoin as a hedge against inflation and economic instability. As a result, companies are diversifying their portfolios by allocating a portion of their reserves to Bitcoin, thereby legitimizing its status in traditional finance. This trend is likely to continue, further embedding Bitcoin within the global financial system.

Another critical insight is the ongoing development of regulatory frameworks surrounding Bitcoin. Governments worldwide are grappling with how to regulate cryptocurrencies, balancing the need for consumer protection and financial stability with the desire to foster innovation. As regulations become clearer, they will likely influence Bitcoin's adoption and integration into mainstream finance. However, the challenge remains in creating regulations that do not stifle innovation while ensuring that the ecosystem is secure and trustworthy for users.

Technological advancements represent another key area of insight. Innovations such as the Lightning Network, which enables faster and cheaper transactions, are crucial for addressing Bitcoin's scalability issues. These developments not only enhance Bitcoin's usability but also position it as a viable medium of exchange for everyday transactions. Additionally, the introduction of various tools and platforms that enhance Bitcoin's security and user experience will be pivotal in attracting a broader audience, thus driving further adoption.

Lastly, the evolving narrative surrounding Bitcoin as a form of digital gold underscores its potential in the investment landscape. As more individuals seek alternative stores of value amid economic uncertainty, Bitcoin's unique properties—such as its limited supply and decentralized nature—make it an appealing option. The perception of Bitcoin as a safeguard against traditional financial risks may encourage more people to explore its investment potential, leading to increased interest and engagement within the cryptocurrency market.

In summary, the insights gathered from Bitcoin's ongoing journey highlight a complex interplay of institutional adoption, regulatory development, technological advancements, and evolving narratives. For adults keen on understanding Bitcoin's future, these factors will play a critical role in shaping its next chapter. By staying informed about these dynamics, individuals can better position themselves to navigate the challenges and opportunities that lie ahead in the world of Bitcoin.

The Road Ahead for Bitcoin

The future of Bitcoin, often perceived as a digital gold, is poised to evolve significantly as it faces a myriad of innovations and challenges. As we look ahead, it is essential to understand the potential pathways that Bitcoin might take, influenced by technological advancements, regulatory developments, and shifting market dynamics. This subchapter explores the various factors that could shape the trajectory of Bitcoin, examining both opportunities and obstacles that lie ahead.

One of the most significant innovations on the horizon is the improvement of Bitcoin's scalability. Current challenges related to transaction speed and cost have led to increased interest in second-layer solutions such as the Lightning Network. This technology allows for faster, cheaper transactions by creating off-chain channels that can settle back to the main blockchain. As these solutions become more robust and widely adopted, they could enhance Bitcoin's usability for everyday transactions, thereby expanding its role as a medium of exchange rather than just a store of value.

In addition to technological developments, regulatory landscapes will play a crucial role in Bitcoin's future. Governments around the world are grappling with how to approach cryptocurrencies, leading to a patchwork of regulations that can either foster innovation or stifle it. Countries that embrace a forward-thinking regulatory framework may attract crypto businesses and investors, creating an environment conducive to growth. Conversely, restrictive measures could push innovation underground or encourage the development of alternative cryptocurrencies. The balance that regulators strike will significantly influence Bitcoin's acceptance and integration into the global financial system.

Market dynamics also present both opportunities and challenges for Bitcoin's future. As institutional interest grows, evidenced by the increasing number of companies adding Bitcoin to their balance sheets or offering cryptocurrency services, Bitcoin may gain legitimacy as an asset class. However, this influx of institutional investment could also lead to increased volatility as traditional financial practices clash with the unique nature of cryptocurrencies. The interplay between supply and demand, especially in response to macroeconomic factors such as inflation and monetary policy, will continue to shape Bitcoin's price and overall market sentiment.

Another critical factor in Bitcoin's journey is the ongoing debate surrounding its environmental impact. Bitcoin mining has been criticized for its significant energy consumption, prompting calls for more sustainable practices within the industry. As awareness of climate issues grows, the Bitcoin community faces pressure to adopt greener technologies, such as renewable energy sources or more energy-efficient mining methods. The industry's ability to address these concerns could determine public perception and regulatory responses, influencing Bitcoin's long-term viability.

In conclusion, the road ahead for Bitcoin is filled with both promise and uncertainty. Innovations in technology and solutions to scalability issues can enhance Bitcoin's utility, while regulatory approaches and market dynamics will shape its adoption and integration into the mainstream economy. Addressing environmental concerns will be pivotal in securing Bitcoin's future as a responsible and sustainable financial alternative. As stakeholders navigate these challenges, the potential for Bitcoin to become a fundamental component of the global financial landscape remains within reach, dependent on the choices made today.

Encouraging Responsible Engagement with Bitcoin

Encouraging responsible engagement with Bitcoin is essential as the cryptocurrency ecosystem continues to evolve and mature. As more individuals seek to understand and participate in Bitcoin, it becomes crucial to foster a culture of responsibility and informed decision-making. This subchapter will explore the significance of education, the importance of security practices, and the role of community engagement in promoting responsible use of Bitcoin.

Education serves as the cornerstone of responsible engagement with Bitcoin. Many newcomers are drawn to Bitcoin by its potential for financial gain, but a lack of understanding can lead to poor investment choices and heightened risk. Comprehensive educational resources, including online courses, webinars, and community workshops, can equip individuals with the knowledge necessary to navigate the complexities of the cryptocurrency market. By focusing on key topics such as blockchain technology, market volatility, and the regulatory landscape, individuals can make informed decisions that align with their financial goals and risk tolerance.

Security practices are another critical component of responsible engagement. As Bitcoin transactions are irreversible and the potential for loss due to hacking or fraud is significant, users must prioritize the protection of their digital assets. This includes utilizing hardware wallets, enabling two-factor authentication, and being vigilant about phishing attempts. Educating users on these best practices not only safeguards individual investments but also contributes to the overall integrity of the Bitcoin network. A secure environment fosters confidence, encouraging more people to engage with Bitcoin while minimizing the risks associated with its use.

Community engagement plays a vital role in promoting responsible Bitcoin use. By cultivating open discussions and sharing experiences, individuals can learn from one another and develop a collective understanding of both the potential rewards and risks associated with Bitcoin. Local meetups, online forums, and social media groups provide platforms for users to exchange ideas, seek advice, and offer support. This sense of community not only enhances individual knowledge but also reinforces a culture of responsibility and ethical behavior within the Bitcoin ecosystem.

Lastly, encouraging responsible engagement requires a proactive approach from stakeholders, including developers, educators, and industry leaders. Initiatives aimed at fostering transparency and ethical standards can help guide users toward responsible practices. By creating frameworks that prioritize user protection, ethical investment strategies, and sustainable development, the Bitcoin community can ensure that its growth benefits everyone involved. As Bitcoin continues to evolve, embracing responsible engagement will be crucial in shaping its future and ensuring that it remains a viable and trustworthy financial alternative for all.

Chapter 10: Resources for Further Exploration

Recommended Reading

In the rapidly evolving landscape of cryptocurrency, particularly Bitcoin, staying informed is essential for both enthusiasts and investors. "Bitcoin's Next Chapter: Innovations and Challenges Ahead" aims to equip readers with insights into the future trajectory of Bitcoin, making recommended reading an invaluable resource. This subchapter highlights key texts that explore various dimensions of Bitcoin, from its technical foundations to its socio-economic implications.

One of the most foundational texts in understanding Bitcoin is "Mastering Bitcoin" by Andreas M. Antonopoulos. This book serves as an in-depth guide to the technical workings of Bitcoin, making it accessible even for those without a computer science background. Antonopoulos breaks down complex concepts into digestible segments, providing readers with a clear understanding of how Bitcoin operates at a technical level. His emphasis on decentralization and the potential for blockchain technology to disrupt traditional financial systems makes it a crucial read for anyone looking to grasp the core principles of Bitcoin and its underlying architecture.

For those interested in the economic implications of Bitcoin, "The Bitcoin Standard" by Saifedean Ammous is a must-read. This book explores Bitcoin's role as a new form of digital gold and its potential to serve as a hedge against inflation. Ammous delves into the historical context of sound money and its importance in fostering economic stability. He argues that Bitcoin's finite supply and decentralized nature make it a viable alternative to fiat currencies, offering readers a thought-provoking perspective on the future of money. This exploration of Bitcoin's economic significance is essential for understanding its potential impact on global financial systems.

Another important addition to the recommended reading list is "Digital Gold" by Nathaniel Popper. This narrative-driven account chronicles the history of Bitcoin and the people who have shaped its journey. Popper's storytelling approach not only provides historical context but also humanizes the technology by highlighting the motivations and challenges faced by early adopters and innovators in the Bitcoin space. This book is particularly valuable for readers who appreciate a more narrative-driven exploration of Bitcoin's evolution, making it easier to connect with the broader implications of this revolutionary technology.

Lastly, "The Basics of Bitcoins and Blockchains" by Antony Lewis offers a practical guide for those looking to understand the mechanics of Bitcoin and other cryptocurrencies. Lewis provides straightforward explanations of complex topics such as wallets, exchanges, and the broader implications of blockchain technology. This book is particularly useful for readers who may not have a technical background but are eager to engage with the cryptocurrency market. By demystifying the jargon often associated with Bitcoin, Lewis empowers readers to make informed decisions in an increasingly digital financial landscape.

In conclusion, the recommended reading list serves as a vital companion to "Bitcoin's Next Chapter: Innovations and Challenges Ahead." By engaging with these texts, readers not only enhance their understanding of Bitcoin but also position themselves to navigate its future developments effectively. Whether through technical insights, economic analyses, historical context, or practical guides, these books collectively offer a comprehensive foundation for anyone interested in the ongoing evolution of Bitcoin and its potential to reshape the financial world.

Online Communities and Forums

Online communities and forums have become pivotal spaces for discussions surrounding Bitcoin and its future. As the cryptocurrency landscape evolves, these digital platforms foster a sense of belonging and engagement among enthusiasts, investors, and newcomers alike. From Reddit threads to specialized Discord servers, these communities serve as vital resources for sharing knowledge, discussing innovations, and addressing challenges associated with Bitcoin. They not only facilitate the exchange of ideas but also support the development of a collective understanding of this complex technology.

One of the most significant advantages of online communities is the diversity of perspectives they offer. Participants come from various backgrounds, including technology, finance, academia, and everyday users. This variety enriches the discourse, allowing members to explore Bitcoin from multiple angles. For instance, developers may share insights on scaling solutions and security protocols, while investors might discuss market trends and investment strategies. Such discussions can lead to a deeper understanding of Bitcoin's potential and the challenges it faces, fostering a more informed community.

Moreover, online forums often serve as incubators for innovation. Many Bitcoin-related projects and initiatives are born from conversations that begin in these spaces. For example, decentralized finance (DeFi) concepts and layer-two scaling solutions have gained traction through collaborative discussions on platforms like Bitcoin Talk and GitHub. These forums allow for real-time feedback and iteration, enabling developers and entrepreneurs to refine their ideas based on community input. As a result, the dynamic nature of these communities can accelerate the pace of innovation, shaping the future of Bitcoin and its ecosystem.

However, navigating the vast sea of information in online communities can be challenging. Misinformation and speculation often circulate, leading to confusion and potentially harmful decisions. It is essential for participants to critically evaluate the information shared within these forums, cross-referencing it with reputable sources and expert opinions. Community moderators and experienced members play a crucial role in maintaining the quality of discussions, identifying misleading content, and fostering an atmosphere of constructive dialogue. This vigilance is vital for ensuring that the community remains a trustworthy resource for all participants.

In conclusion, online communities and forums are indispensable components of the Bitcoin landscape. They provide a platform for knowledge sharing, foster innovation, and facilitate discourse among diverse stakeholders. As Bitcoin continues to evolve, these digital spaces will be instrumental in shaping its trajectory, addressing challenges, and exploring new opportunities. Engaging with these communities can empower individuals to become informed participants in the ongoing dialogue about Bitcoin's future, ultimately contributing to the cryptocurrency's growth and adoption in the broader financial ecosystem.

Educational Platforms and Courses

In recent years, the proliferation of educational platforms dedicated to Bitcoin and cryptocurrency has transformed the way individuals engage with digital currencies. These platforms serve as vital resources for those looking to deepen their understanding of Bitcoin's underlying technology, economic implications, and potential future developments. From structured courses provided by universities to online platforms that offer self-paced learning, the diversity in educational offerings reflects the growing interest in Bitcoin as both an investment vehicle and a technological innovation.

Many traditional educational institutions have recognized the importance of incorporating cryptocurrency into their curricula. Universities and colleges are now offering specialized courses that cover blockchain technology, cryptocurrency trading, and the regulatory landscape surrounding digital currencies. These courses often feature expert instructors who provide students with a comprehensive understanding of how Bitcoin functions within the broader financial ecosystem. By integrating Bitcoin education into academic programs, these institutions are preparing a new generation of professionals who will navigate the complexities of the cryptocurrency market.

Online learning platforms have also emerged as significant players in the educational landscape surrounding Bitcoin. Websites like Coursera, Udemy, and Khan Academy host a variety of courses aimed at different skill levels, from beginners to advanced practitioners. These platforms allow learners to access materials from anywhere in the world, making it easier for individuals to acquire knowledge at their own pace. Additionally, many of these courses are designed to be interactive, featuring quizzes, forums, and peer discussions that enhance the learning experience and promote a deeper understanding of the subject matter.

Moreover, industry-specific training programs are being developed to address the unique challenges and opportunities presented by Bitcoin. Organizations such as the Blockchain Training Alliance and the Cryptocurrency Certification Consortium offer certifications aimed at professionals seeking to validate their skills in blockchain technology and cryptocurrency management. These programs not only provide theoretical knowledge but also practical applications, equipping participants with the tools necessary to succeed in a rapidly evolving industry. As the demand for qualified professionals continues to rise, these training programs play a critical role in shaping the future workforce.

The importance of educational platforms and courses in the realm of Bitcoin cannot be overstated. As the cryptocurrency landscape continues to evolve, staying informed about technological advancements, regulatory changes, and market dynamics is crucial for anyone involved in the space. By leveraging the resources available through educational institutions and online platforms, individuals can better understand the potential of Bitcoin and its implications for the future of finance. This knowledge is not only empowering but also essential for navigating the complexities of a digital economy that is increasingly driven by innovation and technological change.

Thanks for reading.

www.ingramcontent.com/pod-product-compliance
Lightning Source LLC
Chambersburg PA
CBHW071102240526
45471CB00016B/2490